BIOGRAPHIC
DIOR

BIOGRAPHIC
DIOR

LIZ FLAVELL

AMMONITE
PRESS

First published 2017 by
Ammonite Press
an imprint of Guild of Master Craftsman Publications Ltd
Castle Place, 166 High Street, Lewes, East Sussex, BN7 1XU,
United Kingdom
www.ammonitepress.com

ISBN 978 1 78145 313 1

A catalogue record for this book is available from the
British Library.

Publisher: Jason Hook
Concept Design: Matt Carr
Design & Illustration: Matt Carr & Robin Shields
Editor: Jamie Pumfrey
Consultant Editor: NJ Stevenson

Colour reproduction by GMC Reprographics
Printed and bound in Turkey

CONTENTS

ICONOGRAPHIC

WHEN WE CAN RECOGNIZE A FASHION DESIGNER BY A SET OF ICONS, WE CAN ALSO RECOGNIZE HOW COMPLETELY THAT DESIGNER AND THEIR WORK HAVE ENTERED OUR CULTURE AND OUR CONSCIOUSNESS.

INTRODUCTION

Mention Christian Dior and the chances are that you will think of exquisite clothes, fine perfumes and high-end accessories which adorn celebrities, princesses and the girlfriends of Russian oligarchs. The 'CD' monogram that dangles from expensive handbags or adorns belts and glasses is synonymous with the luxury brand rather than the French fashion designer that revolutionized women's clothes in the 1940s and 1950s.

In 1956, Christian Dior wrote, "There are two Christian Diors." And for him this was true; for he was referring to the public figure and the private individual, which is how the somewhat reclusive couturier came to think of himself. There is a certain duality about the name still, but these days it is because the brand is as famous as its creator. However, until we understand Christian Dior the man, how can we ever hope to know the complexities of this exalted heritage brand?

"IN 1947, IT WAS TIME FOR FASHION TO FORSAKE ADVENTURE AND MAKE A TEMPORARY RETURN TO BASE."

—Christian Dior, *Dior by Dior*, 1957

The House of Dior has always created a stir in the fashion world. Head designer Yves Saint Laurent and his triangular 'trapeze' dresses caused a buzz in the late 1950s. Artistic director and 'enfant terrible' John Galliano took haute couture beyond its wildest dreams when he took the reins in 1996. In 2015, Dior still had the power to make history by making Rihanna its first black fashion ambassador. And, in 2017, Dior employed its first woman, the Italian designer Maria Chiuri, as artistic director. But, the most poignant moment in its story remains that day in 1947 when Christian Dior unleashed his first collection on the world ...

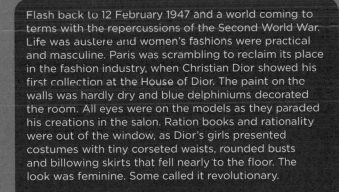

Flash back to 12 February 1947 and a world coming to terms with the repercussions of the Second World War. Life was austere and women's fashions were practical and masculine. Paris was scrambling to reclaim its place in the fashion industry, when Christian Dior showed his first collection at the House of Dior. The paint on the walls was hardly dry and blue delphiniums decorated the room. All eyes were on the models as they paraded his creations in the salon. Ration books and rationality were out of the window, as Dior's girls presented costumes with tiny corseted waists, rounded busts and billowing skirts that fell nearly to the floor. The look was feminine. Some called it revolutionary.

The iconic 'Bar' suit was the highlight of the show and remains the costume that defines what is called the 'New Look'. At heart, Christian was traditional and wanted to bring back romanticism after the war. Since then, the Bar suit has been reinvented by consecutive artistic directors at the House of Dior. And, to this day, they have gone through the archives and reinterpreted Christian's classic designs or paid homage to him in some way.

At the heart of everything that happens at the House of Dior is the spirit of its creator – the genius of Christian Dior permeates each and every collection. Raf Simons festooned delphiniums on the set of his spring/summer 2016 show, paraded necklaces with the number 47 and reworked the Bar jacket as a knit. In 2017, Maria Chiuri created evening dresses embroidered with emblems from the tarot cards in which Christian Dior placed so much faith. The same year, she created a whole collection in navy in homage to Christian and his love of the colour. Just as Christian reached back in time to seek inspiration, the creative team at Christian Dior continues to keep the past ever present and ensure luxury lives on ...

"SUDDENLY I COME TO VIEW MY OTHER SELF WITH GENUINE RESPECT, PERHAPS THE WRETCHED COUTURIER HAS SOMETHING TO BE SAID FOR HIM AFTER ALL ... HIS ROLE IS TO BE A GUARDIAN OF THE PUBLIC TASTE – AND THAT IS A VALUABLE ROLE INDEED."

—Christian Dior, *Dior by Dior*, 1957

CHRISTIAN DIOR

01
LIFE

"WOMEN HAVE INSTINCTIVELY UNDERSTOOD THAT I DREAM OF MAKING THEM NOT ONLY MORE BEAUTIFUL, BUT ALSO HAPPIER. THAT IS WHY THEY HAVE REWARDED ME WITH THEIR PATRONAGE."

—Christian Dior, *Dior by Dior*, 1957

CHRISTIAN DIOR

was born on 21 January 1905
in Granville, France

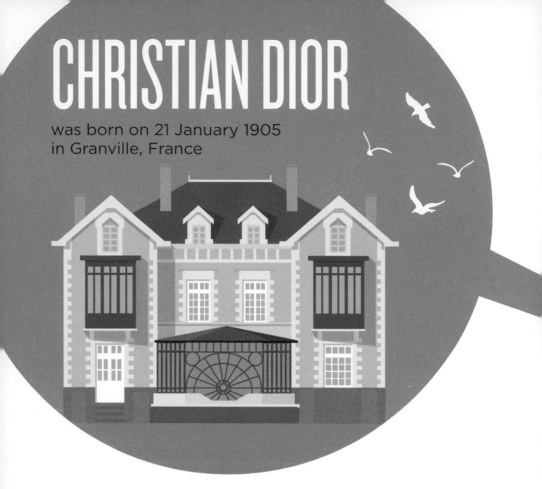

Christian Dior was born in the seaside town of Granville in Normandy, France. The second child of Alexandre Louis Maurice Dior and Marie Madeleine Juliette Martin, he had an idyllic childhood. The family lived in Les Rhumbs (above), a pretty pink villa perched on the cliffs near the fashionable seaside resort. Madame Dior adored gardening and the grounds of Les Rhumbs tumbled with beautiful blooms.

Maurice Dior had made his fortune in fertilizer. When the locals said the streets "smell of Dior", they were referring to the stench of seagull excrement (guano) that wafted from the fertilizer factory that belonged to the Diors.

GRANVILLE

In its fashionable heyday, Granville was known as 'the Monaco of the north'. Now fashionistas head to the Normandy town to visit the Christian Dior Museum at his childhood home, Les Rhumbs.

FRANCE

ON CHRISTIAN DIOR'S BIRTHDAY ...

21 JANUARY

1924 Benny Hill, English comedian, is born.

1924 Vladimir Lenin, communist revolutionary and Russian leader, dies.

1940 Jack Nicklaus, Masters-winning golfer, is born.

1941 Plácido Domingo, Spanish opera tenor, is born.

1950 George Orwell, English novelist, dies.

1970 The Boeing 747 sets off on its first commercial flight between New York and London.

1976 Concorde makes its first commercial flights; London Heathrow to Bahrain and Paris to Rio de Janeiro.

1979 Neptune becomes the outermost planet in the solar system when Pluto crosses its orbit.

2013 Michael Winner, British film director, dies.

THE WORLD IN 1905

15 MAY, USA

Las Vegas is founded as a railroad town, after the 110 acre plot of land, upon which the main strip will later be built, is sold at auction.

4 MARCH, USA

Theodore 'Teddy' Roosevelt begins his second term as president. His first term began in 1901 after the assassination of President McKinley, when, aged 42, he became the youngest president of the United States.

22 JANUARY, RUSSIA

The Russian Revolution of 1905 becomes violent when troops fire at unarmed demonstrators in St Petersburg. Around 200 people, including women and children, are killed and 800 are injured on what becomes known as Red Sunday. The Revolution rages until July 1907.

I JULY, SWITZERLAND

The German physicist Albert Einstein publishes his groundbreaking special theory of relativity. Einstein's theory changes the understanding of physics and astronomy. Later in the year, he creates his famous formula $E=mc^2$.

STARS OF THE SILVER SCREEN BORN IN 1905 ...

Robert Donat: 18 March
Joan Crawford: 23 March
Joseph Cotten: 15 May
Henry Fonda: 16 May
Clara Bow: 29 July
Greta Garbo: 18 September

THE DIOR FAMILY

Maurice Dior was a French industrialist and the owner of a successful chemical fertilizer business. In 1898, at the age of 26, he married Madeleine Martin, who was six years his junior. The couple moved to Granville, where Maurice had grown up, and had five children.

Madeleine was strict and stylish. Christian was her pet and she was his inspiration. She hoped her son would marry the daughter of an English army colonel who lived in Granville; she never suspected her son was gay. Christian never married or had children. Eventually, his fashion house became his family, and he often referred to his models as "mes enfants".

Lily of the valley was one of Christian and his mother's favourite flowers.

MOTHER

Marie Madeleine Juliette Martin (1879–1931)

BROTHER

Raymond Dior (1899–1967)

Christian Dior (1905–57)

Christian never forgot his brother's childish pranks, such as locking him in the cellar or pushing bugs under his bedroom door. As a result of the torment, Christian later wrote Raymond out of his will.

FATHER

Alexandre Louis
Maurice Dior
(1872–1946)

Catherine was a member of the French
Resistance. Christian named the
perfume Miss Dior after his little sister.

SISTER

Jacqueline Dior
(1909–unknown)

BROTHER

Bernard Dior
(1910–60)

SISTER

Ginette
(aka Catherine)
Dior
(1917–2008)

Christian's little brother was
declared mentally ill in 1930 and
was institutionalized until his death.

CHILDHOOD INSPIRATION

Les Rhumbs and the streets of Granville fired the imagination of the somewhat solitary boy ...

CARNIVAL AND COSTUMES

The Granville carnival was the highlight of the year for Christian. The masked balls were an opportunity to dress up all the family. Whether it was Harlequin or King Neptune, his costumes were always inventive.

THINK GREY AND PINK

Les Rhumbs had a facade of soft pink mixed with grey gravelling. Christian used the colour combination extensively in his couture and to decorate the interior at the House of Dior.

FLOWER POWER

Christian poured over plant catalogues and learned the names and descriptions of flowers by heart.

BOOKS AT BEDTIME

Picture books like *Michel Strogoff* and *Around the World in Eighty Days* were Christian's favourites. The 'Nautilus' from *Twenty Thousand Leagues Under the Sea* inspired a love of engineering.

AROUND THE WORLD

IN EIGHTY DAYS

THE LINEN ROOM

Hanging around the housemaids and seamstresses, Christian learned how to use a sewing machine and made costumes for the carnival.

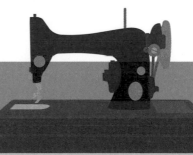

YOUNG DIOR

GRANVILLE 1905

1912

Business was booming for Dior and Sons, and Maurice moved the family to a grand apartment on Rue Albéric-Magnard in Paris. Christian enjoyed all that *Belle Époque* Paris had to offer. The 'last age of elegance' saw fashions, with the use of corsets, develop more elongated, straight silhouettes. During this time, Christian began to accompany his mother to dress fittings.

1914

At school in Paris, Christian was a good pupil with one bad habit – doodling outlines of women wearing high heels on the covers of his school books. After the outbreak of the First World War, the Dior family retreated to Granville. Christian was appalled by the latest fashions in Paris.

1919

After the war, the family returned to Paris but it had changed. Aged 14, Christian found the call of the New Age, which included Cubist art and jazz music, irresistible. His school grades suffered, but at the bar of Le Boeuf sur le Toit, alongside drinkers and thinkers such as Picasso, Cocteau and Satie, he received an entirely different education.

> "I LOOKED AT WOMEN, ADMIRED THE SHAPE OF THEM, WAS AWARE OF THEIR ELEGANCE LIKE ALL BOYS MY AGE, BUT I SHOULD HAVE BEEN VERY MUCH ASTONISHED IF ANYONE HAD PROPHESIED THAT ONE DAY I SHOULD BE A DRESS DESIGNER."

—Christian Dior, *Je Suis Couturier*, 1951

1923

Christian was a young bohemian with aspirations of being an architect. His parents refused to fund the idea, wanting him instead to become a diplomat. Christian enrolled at the Paris Institute of Political Studies as a compromise. Meanwhile, he spent his nights doing exactly as he liked at theatres, bars, balls, galleries and parties with creative cronies such as the composer Henri Sauguet, painter Christian Bérard and poet-painter Max Jacob.

1925

At the Exposition Internationale des Arts Décoratifs of 1925, Christian had a major revelation. Paul Poiret, the current 'King of Fashion', had installed three barges on the Seine, decorated in patriotic red, white and blue, and used them to showcase his collections. Couture and creativity were united in his beautiful displays. Until Poiret, dressmaking was not considered an art. For the first time, Christian envisioned how the two worlds could collide ...

THE GAME OF LIFE

By 1928, it was clear that a diplomat's life was not for Christian. He persuaded his parents to finance an art gallery in Paris instead. It was chance that eventually led to his career in couture ...

1928

Christian's parents finance an art gallery but insist that the Dior name does not appear above the door. Christian opens the gallery with his good friend Jacques Bonjean and names it after him, selling works by Picasso, Braque, Dalí et al.

1938

Swiss couturier Robert Piguet gives Christian his first full-time job as assistant designer. Paris socialite Marie-Louise Bousquet introduces him as 'one to watch' to the editor of *Harper's Bazaar*.

1936

Christian's career as a fashion illustrator and designer takes off as he freelances for Balenciaga, Nina Ricci, Schiaparelli and Patou, among others. He moves into a new apartment at 10 rue Royale.

1939

The Second World War begins and Christian gets his call-up papers. He is a Soldat première classe (Private first class) with the Génie (Engineers) regiment. Later, Germans occupy Paris and Christian is demobbed.

1940

Christian spends 18 months in the village of Callian in the South of France, where he takes up market gardening.

1941

Paris is still occupied, but Christian returns to his Parisian home at rue Royale.

1930

A mirror smashes to the floor at Les Rhumbs. Being superstitious, Christian believes it means seven years of bad luck. That year his younger brother Bernard is declared insane and placed in an asylum.

1931

Christian's mother dies, she is 51 years old. The cause of death is recorded as septicaemia but the family believe that grief for Bernard is really her undoing.

The Dior fertilizer business suffers hard times, and the family loses everything. Later in the year, Christian's partner Jacques is ruined and the gallery is closed.

MARIE
MADELEINE
JULIETTE
MARTIN

1879–1931

1935

Christian moves into the Paris home of fashion illustrator Jean Ozenne. Jean teaches him how to sketch and sells some of Christian's illustrations. Christian is inspired and perfects his art.

1934

Christian is struck down with tuberculosis. His close friends pay for him to recuperate in a sanitorium in Ibiza where he discovers tapestry weaving and finds a desire to 'do' something with his hands.

1942

Christian works alongside the designer Pierre Balmain at the House of Lucien Lelong. Lelong, as president of the Chambre Syndicale de la Couture Parisienne, had persuaded the Nazis not to move the Paris fashion industry to Berlin during the Occupation. The only clients for Parisian Couture were German, but Lelong contrived to keep business active and 90 Couture houses were able to stay open.

1946

Christian is offered the position of Artistic Director at the House of Philippe et Gaston. After stumbling on a 'lucky star' on the pavement, Christian believes it is a sign to refuse the job, go solo and create the House of Dior ...

THE NEW LOOK

Maison Christian Dior opened its doors on 16 December 1946. On 12 February 1947, 90 different looks were paraded before the fashion elite at the famous home of couture, to rave reviews ...

"IT'S QUITE A REVOLUTION, DEAR CHRISTIAN. YOUR DRESSES HAVE SUCH A NEW LOOK."

—Carmel Snow, editor of *Harper's Bazaar*, in a letter to Christian Dior a few days after the debut show, 1947

CONTROVERSY

Not everyone was so enamoured with the collection, and many saw the New Look as unpatriotic due to the large amount of fabric used in a time of shortages. In Montmartre, mannequins wearing the outfits for a *Vogue* photoshoot were pelted with fruit by market stallholders.

"A SENSATIONAL SUCCESS ..."

—*Harper's Bazaar*, 1947

"MY FIRST COLLECTION WAS SUCCESSFUL BEYOND MY WILDEST DREAM."

—Christian Dior,
Dior by Dior, 1957

"[I WAS AWARE] OF AN ELECTRIC TENSION THAT I HAD NEVER BEFORE FELT IN THE COUTURE."

—Bettina Ballard describing the first show, *American Vogue*, 1947

DIOR'S FIRSTS

Christian's fashion revolution lasted until his death in 1957. He enjoyed ten years at the top and was often first.

1957

Christian becomes the first French couturier to appear on the cover of *Time* magazine.

TIME

CHRISTIAN DIOR

1956

The fragrance Diorissimo is first issued.

1955

Christian hires Yves Saint Laurent as his assistant. The first ready-to-wear shoes designed by Charles Jourdan are launched. Dior Perfumes creates its first major range of make-up with 22 lipsticks. Henkel & Grosse takes on the first licence for Christian Dior Jewellery.

1954

Christian holds a fashion show at Blenheim Palace, England, at the invitation of the Duchess of Marlborough and before Princess Margaret. The first de-luxe ready-to-wear shop opens in London.

1947

Dior's first collection features the iconic 'Bar' suit. The first perfume, Miss Dior, is launched. Christian Dior Furs is created.

1949

The first advertising campaign for Dior Perfumes, which includes Diorama, is released.

1950

Christian is the first designer to license his name to luxury items such as handbags and scarves. The first men's accessories, Christian Dior Ties and Cravats, are launched. Christian makes his first and only trip to the United States.

1953

Dior launch their first lipstick, Rouge Dior. The first Dior shop in Caracas, Venezuela, is opened. Together with Roger Vivier, Christian creates the first made-to-measure Dior shoe.

DIOR BY NUMBERS

FAVOURITE SIBLING

Christian had two brothers and two sisters but Ginette, later known as Catherine, was his favourite. She gave him the nickname Tian. In turn, his favourite day was St Catherine's Day. She was named a Chevalier of the Legion d'Honneur for her work with the resistance in the Second World War.

3 BOOKS

Christian self-penned books so he could put the record right about his life and work.

8 LUCKY NUMBER

Christian gave one of his debut lines the name '8' because the tiny waist, the enhanced hips and the bigger bust looked a little like the figure eight.

The House of Dior was founded in the 8th arrondissement of Paris, in an eight-storey building with eight workshops, on 8 October 1946.

I AM A COUTURIER (1951)

THE LITTLE DICTIONARY OF FASHION: A GUIDE TO DRESS SENSE FOR EVERY WOMAN (1954)

DIOR BY DIOR: THE AUTO-BIOGRAPHY OF CHRISTIAN DIOR (1957)

87 COUNTRIES

By 1957, Christian Dior had conquered the world, with licences issued to places as far flung as Australia, USA, Canada, Cuba and Britain.

12 DRESSES

Movie stars adored gowns by Monsieur Dior. In 1956, Christian designed at least a dozen dresses for the actress Ava Gardner for her film *The Little Hut*.

100,000 CREATIONS

By 1956, the 10th anniversary of the House of Dior, the company had created thousands of garments and was turning over $20 million a year.

DEATH OF DIOR

A LIFE OF EXCESS

Ten years of leading the House of Dior took its toll on Christian's health. He adored food and he used chocolates to assuage stress. By 1957, Christian was overweight and regularly breathless, and he'd had a bed installed in an anteroom at work so he could rest.

24 OCTOBER 1957

In the autumn of 1957, while on a short break at the Italian spa town of Montecatini, Christian Dior died. After dinner and a game of canasta, he collapsed with a heart attack. He was just 52 years old.

FLOWERS FOR CHRISTIAN

Hours after his death, the windows at Maison Christian Dior were draped in black velvet. Soon there were so many flowers piled up at the doors that the government granted an unprecedented honour, allowing the flowers to be distributed along the route to the Arc de Triomphe.

Christian is buried at the cemetery at Callian in the South of France. He shares a vault with his father Maurice and mother Madeleine. The Neo-Romantic sculpture was designed by Christian. They rest together under the cypress trees.

CHRISTIAN DIOR

02
WORLD

"DIOR IS THAT NIMBLE GENIUS UNIQUE TO OUR AGE WITH THE MAGICAL NAME — COMBINING GOD AND GOLD [DIEU ET OR]."

—Jean Cocteau, from *Christian Dior* by Marie France Pochna, 2009

THE CITY OF LIGHT

Paris was Christian's base all his life. Discover his homes, haunts and other places ...

LUCKY STAR
Rue du Faubourg Saint-Honoré

Christian stumbles upon his lucky star!

HOUSE OF PIGUET
3 Rond-point des Champs-Élysées

Christian's first job in fashion.

GALERIE JACQUES BONJEAN
34 rue La Boétie

Christian sets up the art gallery with his friend Jacques.

DIOR FAMILY RESIDENCE
9 rue Louis David

HOUSE OF DIOR
30 avenue Montaigne

The House of Dior has been located in this impressive building since 1946.

PARIS INSTITUTE OF POLITICAL STUDIES
27 rue Saint-Guillaume

To please his parents, Christian studies here from 1923–26.

CIRQUE MEDRANO
63 boulevard de Rochechouart

Christian and his friends enjoy acts like the Fratellini brothers and Barbette on the trapeze.

THÉÂTRE DES BOUFFES DU NORD
37 bis, boulevard de la Chapelle

This theatre is a regular stomping ground for young Christian.

LE BOEUF SUR LE TOIT
28 rue Boissy d'Anglas

The cabaret bar is a regular haunt for young Christian.

TIP TOES BAR
Rue Tronchet

Christian meets his Bohemian playmates here each week in the 1920s.

CHRISTIAN'S APARTMENT
10 rue Royale

Christian moves here in 1936. During the Second World War, Christian moves to the South of France and returns to the apartment in 1941.

 work

 home

 social

 event

LUCKY MAN

Christian Dior believed in luck and destiny. As a child, he loved to hear his grandmother's prophecies and premonitions. Throughout his life, he was superstitious and looked for signs to help him make the big decisions. When the opportunity arose to open his own couture house, Christian consulted with fortune teller Madam Delahaye. It was her insistence that he take a chance which led to him opening the doors of the House of Dior ...

TAROT CARDS

Before a show, Christian turned to tarot cards to foretell the future. In 2016, Dior's new director Maria Chiuri paid homage to Christian's superstitions with her collection of tarot dresses.

CLOVER

Christian believed in the magical properties of talismans. He carried in his pocket a four-leaf clover, sprigs of lily of the valley and a gold coin.

STAR

Christian stumbled over his lucky star on a Paris pavement. That small, rough, five-pointed star was his sign to start up the House of Dior. Of all his charms and symbols, this was his favourite.

FORTUNE TELLER

Christian used psychics to help him make decisions such as when to show a collection or take a holiday.

UMBRELLA

If anyone dared to enter his office with an umbrella, they were immediately told to leave!

HEART

Two hearts were always stashed in his pocket, alongside his other lucky charms.

LILY OF THE VALLEY

Christian's favourite flower was hidden in the hem of each new garment shown at a collection. Its heady scent is the basis of Dior's iconic fragrance, Diorissimo.

WOOD

Christian had two pieces of wood in his pocket that he would touch before each show and before signing any contract.

WORLD

CONTEMPORARY COUTURIERS

Paris was the epicentre of haute couture throughout the 20th century. The world of fashion is very small and designers were well connected to each other ...

CRISTÓBAL BALENCIAGA
(1895–1972)

Christian Dior called Balenciaga "the master of us all". The Spanish designer was the son of a seamstress and a fisherman. After training as a tailor, he was a successful designer in Spain before the Civil War (1936–9). In 1937, he opened his own couture house in Paris, where he became known for his innovation and as a master of sculptural construction. He was diametrically opposed to Dior's treatment of the female form, creating dresses in conceptual shapes.

HUBERT DE GIVENCHY
(1927–)

The designer who created Audrey Hepburn's famous black dress in *Breakfast at Tiffany's* was born in Beauvais in northern France. At 17, he was an apprentice to Jacques Fath. The House of Givenchy, which he opened in 1952, brought simplicity and chic to the Paris scene. Audrey Hepburn his muse and Balenciaga was his idol. Well known for his 'sack' dress in the 1950s, he embraced the youthful look and raised hemlines in the 1960s.

EDWARD MOLYNEUX
(1891–1974)

JACQUES FATH
(1912–54)

The self-taught fashion designer was born in Paris. In his short lifetime (he died aged 42 of leukemia) he helped to define Parisienne chic. Loved by rich women with sophisticated tastes, he opened the House of Fath in 1947. Young designers like Hubert de Givenchy and Guy Laroche were on his payroll.

ROBERT PIGUET
(1898–1953)

KARL LAGERFELD
(1938–)

LUCIEN LELONG
(1889–1958)

COCO CHANEL
(1883–1971)

In 1926, the French designer Gabrielle 'Coco' Chanel introduced the jersey flapper dress. Corsets and padding played no part in Coco's simple designs. The perfume Chanel No. 5 funded her expansion into jewellery, shoes and other accessories. Coco also said: "Fashion changes, style endures." Her little black dresses and signature suits are testament to that.

YVES SAINT LAURENT
(1936–2008)

PIERRE BALMAIN
(1914–82)

The House of Balmain was opened in 1945. The French-born designer studied architecture in Paris and called dressmaking "the architecture of movement". After dropping out of college, he sketched for Robert Piguet. Later, he worked for Edward Molyneux and Lucien Lelong which is where he met Christian Dior. At the forefront of the 'new French style', his costumes were worn by film stars and royalty. Karl Lagerfeld worked for him for four years before moving on to the House of Jean Patou.

JEAN PATOU
(1887–1936)

THE STARS DRESSED BY DIOR

JOSEPHINE BAKER

A legendary dancer and singer in 1920s Paris, Josephine Baker often wore Dior evening gowns for her stage shows.

MARLENE DIETRICH

Marlene Dietrich, actor and 'symbol of glamour', appeared at the first Dior show in 1947. Dietrich wore Dior in Hitchcock's *Stage Fright*.

EVA PERÓN

As wife of Argentina's President Juan Perón, Eva Perón wanted for nothing; her extensive wardrobe was filled with Dior clothing.

MARGOT FONTEYN

The prima ballerina Margot Fonteyn bought the 'Daisy' suit from the first collection in 1947. She wore a grey silk Dior dress on her wedding day.

LAUREN BACALL

1940s movie star Lauren Bacall was a lifelong fan and was dressed by Dior in *How to Marry a Millionaire*.

MARIA CALLAS

Stylish soprano Maria Callas collaborated with Dior for many of her onstage ensembles.

ÉDITH PIAF

Cabaret singer Édith Piaf chose a Dior wedding gown when she was married in 1952; it was a copy of the dress worn by Marlene Dietrich in *No Highway in the Sky*.

PRINCESS MARGARET

Britain's Princess Margaret wore Dior for her 21st birthday party. Throughout the 1950s she was the royal poster girl for the label.

A LOVE AFFAIR WITH GREAT BRITAIN

ANGLOPHILIA

Christian's love affair began in the English garden his mother created at Les Rhumbs. His anglophilia grew with his visit to England in the 1920s. Enamoured of English manners, British architecture and Anglo style, he learned the language. Of all his Bohemian friends in Paris, Christian was the one who adopted a British look – some would say he had a touch of the Bloomsbury set about him. At the height of his success, he bought English cars.

BRITISH FASHION

Two great English designers, Charles Frederick Worth (1825–95) and Edward Molyneux (1891–1974), right, were major influences on Christian. In the 19th century, royalty and members of the aristocracy frequented the House of Worth in Paris. Worth is credited with being the founder of Parisian haute couture. Christian personally knew Captain Molyneux and admired the Englishman's simplicity, precision and sophistication. They also shared a passion for flowers.

ROYALTY

Hobnobbing with royalty is the icing on the cake for any Anglophile. One of the highlights of Christian's career was a fashion show held at Blenheim Palace in November 1954 before Princess Margaret and 1,600 well-heeled guests. Thirteen models paraded 100 couture pieces and £9,000 was raised for the Red Cross.

CUISINE

Christian loved rich cuisine, especially English food. It is unusual for a French man to dote on stodgy stuff but Christian had a penchant for mince pies, Yorkshire puddings and porridge – as well as eggs and bacon and stuffed chicken. In 1972, *La Cuisine Cousu-Main*, an haute cuisine cookbook by Dior and illustrated by René Gruau, was published. Later in life, he suffered with kidney problems that meant his body couldn't eliminate fatty products. By 1947, he had put on weight and suffered two heart attacks (which he kept secret) but he still indulged in English fayre.

OTHER ANGLOPHILES

Voltaire, Adolf Hitler, John F. Kennedy (right), Tom Cruise, Johnny Depp, Tim Burton, Madonna, Kevin Spacey, Bill Bryson, Loyd Grossman, Terry Gilliam, Elizabeth McGovern.

RULES OF FASHION

In 1954, Christian published his own guide to looking good. Here are some of his timeless tips for fashionistas ...

ON ACCESSORIES ...

"The less you can afford for your frocks, the more care you must take with your accessories. With one frock and different accessories you can always be well turned out."

ON COSMETICS ...

"The most natural make-up is best, and, except for lipstick, it must not show. Brightly coloured nail varnish is all right if you like it, but personally I prefer natural colours."

ON DOTS ...

"Dots are lovely for holiday clothes – cotton frocks and beach outfits – and they are gay, too, for accessories."

ON FEATHERS ...

"Feathers are lovely on a bird and glamorous on a hat, but they must be used with great discrimination. They can look lovely but they can also look ridiculous."

ON LINGERIE ...

"Lovely lingerie is the basis of good dressing."

ON OLDER WOMEN ...

"Nothing is prettier than grey hair. And by the time a woman's hair is grey she has usually acquired a charming kind of dignity and femininity."

ON QUALITY ...

"Quality is essential to elegance. I will always put quality before quantity."

ON SCARVES ...

"A scarf is to a woman what a neck-tie is to a man, and the way you tie it is part of your personality."

ON SILK ...

"The queen of all materials ... You can wear silk from the afternoon until midnight."

ON VARIETY ...

"When you see a woman looking lovely in a beautiful dress you are only too pleased to see her looking like that again."

ON ZEST ...

"Anything you do, work or pleasure, you have to do it with zest. You have to live with zest ... and that is the secret of beauty and fashion, too."

All quotes from The Little Dictionary of Fashion *by Christian Dior, 1954*

Two luxury brands, two inspirational designers, yet so very different. In 1939, Coco Chanel had closed the doors of her fashion house but she made a comeback in 1953 in a bid to end Dior's domination of the fashion scene.

BACKGROUND

The best of everything for the boy born in Granville. Christian dropped out of the Paris Institute of Political Studies.

STYLE

A combination of corsets and clever padding allowed Christian Dior to remodel the female form into what he called a celebration of femininity.

CHRISTIAN DIOR

EARLY DAYS

Christian ran his own modern art gallery in Paris. He sketched for fashion magazines before working as haute couturier at the House of Piguet.

BORN 1905

PALETTE

V

GABRIELLE 'COCO' CHANEL

BORN 1883

PERFECT PERFUME

Chanel No. 5 was launched in 1921.

N°5
CHANEL

BACKGROUND

Coco was born into poverty in a workhouse in Saumur in the Loire Valley. She received a strict convent education.

EARLY DAYS

Coco tried her luck as a singer before launching into fashion as a milliner, gradually turning to designing fresh, casual daywear.

INFLUENCES

Dior reinvented traditional styles. Flowers inspired many lines; the Corolla, Lily of the Valley Line and Tulip Line were ways of creating the ultimate femme-fleur (flower-woman).

PERFECT PERFUME

Miss Dior was launched in 1948.

LASTING LEGACY

The 'New Look' of 1947 became an international brand in its own right.

DIED 1957

52

87

LASTING LEGACY

Chanel's signature suit and the little black dress had enduring appeal.

DIED 1971

STYLE

In the 1920s, Coco Chanel did away with corsets and liberated women with her loose-fitting, short-hemmed, chic and comfortable creations. She used jersey because it hung well and it was excellent value for money.

INFLUENCES

The First World War shook things up for women. Coco looked to menswear and military uniform for inspiration to dress the modern working woman.

THE TWO CHRISTIANS

Christian called his memoirs *Christian Dior et Moi* (published as *Dior by Dior* in English), which refers to the famous design house and himself. There were two sides to the man, too – the successful couturier centred in Paris and the private individual who loved to escape to the country.

WOMEN, WOMEN EVERYWHERE

By 1954, Christian had more than 1,000 employees in Paris, mostly women. He installed strong women at the top who he nicknamed his 'fairy godmothers'. Raymonde Zehnacker was his deputy – she took care of business. Marguerite Carré was his 'Dame Fashion' in charge of sketches. Mitzah Bricard was his muse. The many beautiful brunette models were indulged as if they were his own children.

KIND AND GENTLE

Christian had great respect for everyone that worked for him and created a happy atmosphere that nurtured talent and creativity. At Christmas, each member of staff was given a gift chosen carefully by him. A true gentleman, he always insisted on letting everyone go in front of him into the lift.

SHY STYLE ICON

In 1957, the House of Dior was turning over $20 million a year. That year, Christian became the first designer to grace the cover of *Time* magazine. However, the reclusive couturier rarely met the famous faces who dropped by the House of Dior, and he even refused to make a dress for the actress Brigitte Bardot.

THE PUBLIC FIGURE

THE PRIVATE MAN

UNLUCKY IN LOVE

Christian was doomed to be 'just good friends' with many men, and never found the love he really craved. The Moroccan singer Jacques Benita was his last 'companion', though Christian was more a father figure to the young man than a lover.

THE MIGHTY WORRIER

Behind closed doors there was often stress and insomnia, temper tantrums and tears. Raymonde Zehnacker was there for him round the clock, ready to cajole him or tell him off if he worked too hard or ate too many chocolates.

COUNTRY RETREATS

Weeks away at his country homes were vital to the creative process. Locked away in his bedroom for days, he sketched, schemed and dreamed up the next collection. In later years, he retreated to his cottage in Milly-la-Forêt each weekend. Guests were treated to his homemade fruit cordials.

5 THINGS YOU DIDN'T KNOW ABOUT CHRISTIAN DIOR

1
A fortune teller once predicted that women were lucky for him, they would make him his fortune and he'd travel widely because of them.

2
Christian learned the piano as a boy and always loved to play. He was a close friend of the composer Henri Sauguet. Christian composed a suite of piano pieces he called 'Françaises'.

3
Christian dreamed of being an architect long before he got into fashion. In 1931, he visited the USSR with a party of architects. Russo-Byzantine churches fascinated him.

4
Christian had hundreds of copies made of the lucky star from Rue du Faubourg. These were presented like medals to staff to reward excellence.

5
A coat in each Dior collection is named 'Granville'. More recently the House of Dior has introduced Granville perfume and a collection of jewellery named for his hometown.

CHRISTIAN
DIOR

03
WORK

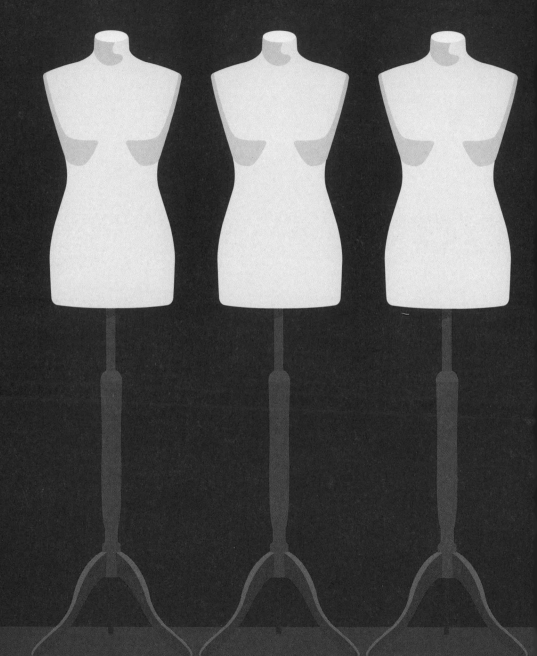

"IN A MACHINE AGE, DRESSMAKING IS ONE OF THE LAST REFUGES OF THE HUMAN, THE PERSONAL, THE INIMITABLE. IN AN EPOCH AS SOMBRE AS OURS, LUXURY MUST BE DEFENDED INCH BY INCH."

—Christian Dior, from *Couture and Commerce* by Alexandra Palmer, 2001

THE CREATIVE PROCESS

01 Merchants from all around the world bring their wares to the House of Dior. Christian selects only the finest from the yards of fabric, lace and other textiles.

02 At least twice a year, Christian disappears to the countryside to work, spending hours in his bathtub 'creating' the next collection.

09 The costumes leave the studio with pins attached and swatches of material trailing.

10 Models are fitted into the costumes at the dress rehearsal in the Grand Salon. Bows and buttons are added, and accessories such as hats, scarves and jewels complete the look. Christian, the patron, has the last say on everything.

03 With a background in fashion illustration, Christian loves to sketch up his ideas:

"A SINGLE SKETCH STARTS OFF A WHOLE SERIES."

04 The sketches are delivered to Paris:

"LIKE SAP, THE CREATIVE IDEA CIRCULATES NOW THROUGHOUT THE WHOLE BUILDING."

08 The final decision – Christian selects costumes for final production. Many creations are rejected at this stage.

05 The team of seamstresses work on the 'toiles' – initial muslin versions of the costumes.

07 Christian selects fabrics for each creation. The costumes are cut, refined, primped and pinned until he is totally satisfied.

06 The toiles are continually reworked until Christian is happy with the result.

ANATOMY OF THE NEW LOOK

Christian's collection of spring 1947 changed fashion
for ever. The question is how, what and why?

JACKET: SHANTUNG JACKET

Q: Have we seen this look before?

A: Yes, Christian loved the elegance of early
20th-century fashion. This shoulder line shouts
1916, so it's not a terribly 'new look' at all.

LONG SKIRT: DEEPLY PLEATED BLACK CLOTH

Q: How low did
those hems go?

A: The skirts dropped
to just over 14 inches
(36 cm) off the ground.

Q: Just how much fabric
was used in those long
flowing skirts?

A: An abundance of fabric.
Sometimes 30, 40 or
even 50 yards (46 m)
of cloth.

Q: How did Dior make the skirts
appear to bloom like flowers?

A: The skirts were lined with
yards of cambric and taffeta
to add body.

Q: What about the hips?
How did he accentuate them?

A: That's down to the padding.
Dior was an 'architect' as
well as a designer.

UP TO 50 YARDS (46 m) OF CLOTH WAS USED IN EACH SKIRT

BUST

Q: The bust looks magnificent. How did he achieve that?

A: To get the rounded look, the basques were built into the dresses. He also insisted his models wore 'falsies'.

WAIST

Q: How did he create those wasp waists?

A: Dior used corsets and whalebone to sculpt the body.

FABRIC

Q: Everything appears so opulent. Which fabrics did he use?

A: Wool, silk, satin – only the most expensive and luxurious.

PRICE TAGS

EVENING DRESS

£340

(£10,000 at today's prices)

NO GARMENTS LESS THAN ...

£100

(£2,500 at today's prices)

GET THE LOOK

Movie stars and royalty were instantly won over by Christian's creations and had the money to indulge themselves, but it wasn't until 1948 that the 'New Look' began to catch on with the general public. For many there was still clothes rationing, so fashionistas invented their own versions of the New Look ...

In Britain, clothing coupons would never allow for the fabric in a Dior-inspired creation. The clothing allowance for the entire year would have been taken up by a single skirt.

Most people didn't have the money to lavish on fashion – £80 for a day dress and upwards of £350 for an evening gown was preposterous!

After the war, the fine fabrics required for mass producing the New Look were in short supply. There was plenty of parachute silk or army khaki but these just didn't cut it for couture.

British dress manufacturers didn't attempt the New Look, but time, ingenuity and sheer demand changed that when they discovered how to get the look without using so much fabric.

1948

Teenagers yearned to achieve the New Look, even if that meant reusing old blackout material to make their own billowing skirts. They perked them up with embroidery, appliqué and even dyeing the material.

King George VI of England didn't want his daughters wearing the New Look. Despite this, the royal couturier added velvet bands to widen and lengthen one of Princess Margaret's coats.

IN THE UK
Butterwick Paper Patterns published an innovative way of taking two old dresses and combining them to create a homemade New Look dress.

IN THE NETHERLANDS
Dutch girls gave the look a real edge by making patchwork New Look skirts. Teamed with US Army T-shirts, they invented a different look entirely.

To lengthen their skirts women often added a panel of material around the waistband then covered it up with a top so nobody could see.

WHAT CHRISTIAN DID NEXT

Over the next decade, Christian invented new ways of highlighting women's curves. Extravagant and opulent, many of his costumes were pure architecture. Each year, new lines were given names that expressed his intention.

1947 Corolle and Back of Paris

1949 Illusion and Foreign Lines

1947	1948	1949	1950	1951
Corolle and Figure of Eight	Zig Zag and Flight	Illusion and Foreign Lines	Vertical Line	Oval Line
Corolle and Back of Paris	Winged Line and Cyclonic Line	Scissor and Windmill Lines	Oblique, Interlaced and Lily of the Valley Lines	Long Line

1953 Living Line

1956 Arrow Line

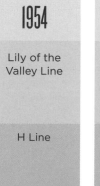

1952	1953	1954	1955	1956
Sinuous Line	Tulip Line	Lily of the Valley Line	A Line	Arrow Line
Profiled Line	Living Line	H Line	Y Line	Magnet Line

'TYRANT OF THE HEMLINES'

When Christian lengthened skirts and other designers followed in his footsteps, he was called 'the tyrant of the hemlines'. Women were quite literally 'hemmed-in' by his impractical designs. In the 1960s, Mary Quant popularized the miniskirt, which allowed women to run for the bus and get groovy! In the last century, how have the hemlines moved?

1912 Modest and demure, skirt lengths mostly hit the floor.

1914 The First World War starts and many designers shorten skirt lengths – the 'wartime crinoline' frees women up to work.

1919 – 29 Straight and knee-length are most popular but, with the flapper, skirt lengths rise higher than ever.

1930s The term 'hemlines' is first introduced. Lean times mean hemlines fall, but Hollywood stars in long evening gowns add glamour to the look.

1940 – 47 During the war years, women needed practical and utilitarian clothes, so neat knee-length is back.

1947 People are shocked by Dior's hemlines that measure just 14 inches (36 cm) from the floor.

1950s Couture is for old ladies, but fashion is for teenagers! Big skirts and petticoats are fun and reveal a well-turned ankle.

1960s

Hems haven't been so high since the 1920s. London designer Mary Quant is often credited with inventing the look and names the new style the 'miniskirt' after the Mini car.

1966

Hemlines hit the upper thigh! Coloured tights are a must-have accessory.

1970s

The new midi and maxi-length dresses, influenced by '70s period films, dominate. Later in the decade, punk rock brings back the shorter skirt.

1980s

The 'rah rah' skirt has more bounce and flounce, but is nearly as short as the mini. Old and new styles collide with Vivienne Westwood's playful 'mini crini'.

1990s

By the end of the 20th century, anything goes!

2000s

Micro-minis or belt skirts worn with leggings are a staple look for western women. The mini still stirs controversy with attempts to ban it in some African countries.

2010s

The mini is considered a more youthful look while Dior's New Look and longer hems are more sophisticated and smart. How women (or men) wear their hemline is down to personal choice.

THE BIG SHOW

The highlight of each collection was the show in the Grand Salon of the House of Dior. The whole team, including a select bunch of Christian's friends, stayed up the night before finishing off and adding final touches to his creations. Exhaustion and expectation were the prelude to excellence ...

"DIOR'S COLLECTION WAS A LONG-AWAITED MOMENT, ON THE SAME SCALE AS THE FIRST NIGHT AT THE OPERA OR A PERFORMANCE BY SOME FANTASTIC ORCHESTRA ..."

—Hélène Rochas

AUTUMN/WINTER 1951

Christian developed one of his favourite looks, the Long line. Inspired by the Princess line, introduced by Frederick Worth in the 19th century, this style hugs the body but relies upon clever cuts, rather than basques and corsets, to achieve shape.

COY CHRISTIAN

Dior was far too shy to be out front watching the reaction of the crowd. Hiding behind a curtain, Christian awaited news from the woman he trusted the most, Raymonde Zehnacker.

EVERY LAST DETAIL

Christian was master of the entire show, even down to all the programme notes, which he wrote himself.

"TO SEE A COLLECTION OF DIOR'S DRESSES FILING PAST GIVES ONE THE PLEASURE OF WATCHING A ROMANTIC AND SPECTACULAR PAGEANT. WITH AN IMPECCABLE TASTE, A HIGHLY CIVILIZED SENSITIVITY AND A RESPECT FOR TRADITION THAT SHOWS ITSELF IN A PREDILECTION FOR THE HALF-FORGOTTEN, DIOR CREATES A BRILLIANT NOSTALGIA."

—Cecil Beaton

DIOR ON COLOUR

BLACK

"The most popular and most convenient and the most elegant of all colours ... It is the most slimming of all colours, and unless you have a bad complexion, it is one of the most flattering."

BLUE

"Amongst all the colours, navy blue is the only one which can ever compete with black ... Be careful when you are selecting a blue to see it both in daylight and electric lights, because it changes very much."

PINK

"The sweetest of all the colours. Every woman should have something pink in her wardrobe."

BROWN

"Together with black, it is one of the best colours for accessories, like handbags, gloves and shoes, because it is a natural colour."

GREY

"The most convenient, useful and elegant neutral colour ... And many people who cannot wear black can wear dark grey. (Remember that if you are big you must choose a dark grey and if you are petite a light grey is better for you.)"

Christian had a natural flair for colour. He felt two colours were enough in any outfit. Mostly he recommended neutral colours with 'touches' of vibrant colour. Colour-planning was vital for the well-dressed woman.

All quotes from The Little Dictionary of Fashion *by Christian Dior, 1954*

GREEN

"It is a colour of nature – and when you follow nature for your colour schemes you can never go far wrong ... There is a green for everyone and for every complexion."

PURPLE

"Purple – king of colours; but it has to be used with great care because it is not young looking. And it is not very gay ..."

RED

"A very energetic and beneficial colour. It is the colour of life ... Bright reds – scarlet, pillar-box red, crimson, cherry are very gay and youthful. And perhaps a red that is a little more sombre is better for the not-so-young – and the not-so-slim, too!"

YELLOW

"The colour of youth and of the sun, and of good weather ... But if you are fair-haired or have a pale complexion you must be afraid of this colour."

WHITE

"White is more beautiful than any colour for evening ... White is pure and simple and matches with everything ... But nothing gives the impression of good grooming and being well dressed more quickly than spotless white ..."

THE H LINE

RESHAPING AGAIN

The flat look took its name from the flattened bustline. And what a change it must have seemed after tiny waists and enhanced bosoms ...

> "I AM NOT BUILT FOR ANY KIND OF BOY'S FASHIONS, SO WHY SHOULD I WEAR THEM?"

—Marilyn Monroe on the H line

THE DEGAS BODICE

The bodice was as flat as the ballet dancer's costume made famous by the Impressionist artist Edgar Degas. It was elegant and refreshing, and offered anyone with a small bosom the opportunity to be redefined and appear more youthful.

"HOW MANY TIMES HAVE I HEARD MEN COMPLAIN THAT, WHILE DANCING, THEY WERE NOT ABLE TO FEEL THE LIVING BODY OF WOMEN UNDER THE YOKE WHICH IMPRISONED THEM."

—Christian Dior, *Time*, 1954

THE TUDOR BODICE

Both romantic and dramatic, the long, close-fitting bodice pushed the bosom up rather like the costumes worn by the ladies in the court of King Henry VIII. Women with a fuller figure would feel younger and more enticing.

MORE DIOR

Christian wanted to dress women in 'Christian Dior' from head to toe. In his lifetime, he saw his name extend to perfumes, fur coats, handbags, shoes, menswear, accessories and beyond.

EAU DE DIOR

Christian once said: "A woman's perfume tells more about her than her handwriting." His love affair with flowers inspired his first fragrance, Miss Dior, in 1947. Diorissimo was launched in 1956 and bursts with the scent of his favourite flower, Lily of the Valley.

IF THE SHOE FITS

A stickler for style, Christian said: "It is by her feet that you can judge whether a woman is elegant or not." In 1953, he collaborated with designer Roger Vivier to create the simple, made-to-measure, quality footwear worthy of his elite customers.

LICENSE TO THRILL

Christian loved expensive leather handbags and believed stylish women should have the right bag for all occasions. A clever businessman, he introduced the concept of licensing to fashion. Christian Dior handbags were made by other producers in return for a percentage of their profits.

DIOR

NEW YORK, NEW STORE

In 1948, Christian Dior New York was opened on Fifth Avenue. The store offered ready-to-wear (prêt-à-porter or off-the-peg) lines with American women in mind.

"I HAD TO UNDERSTAND THE NEEDS OF ELEGANT WOMEN ALL OVER THE WORLD."

—Christian Dior, 1957

FRESH FROM THE BOX

Rich women could leave the Dior boutique on 30 avenue Montaigne drenched in Dior perfume and fully kitted out in his attire. By 1957, scarves, jewellery, hats, stockings and more had the coveted Dior label. Everything went home in a delightful box emblazoned with the logo and tied with ribbon.

5 FACTS ABOUT DIOR'S DRESSES

01 Christian liked to cuddle the fabric he used in his precious creations, so he got a real feel for its flow and form.

02 Each and every dress was filed with a sketch and its number.

03 In November each year, 15-minute appointments were made with textile houses, corsetieres, jewellers, button-makers, belt-makers, milliners and other suppliers so they could parade their wares before Dior.

04 Cotton was considered beneath haute couture, so Christian waited until 1950 before using this 'cheap' fabric in his collections. However, when he made his delightful afternoon dresses in printed cotton, the trend soon caught on.

05 The Spindle line of 1957 would be Christian's final curtain. Loose-fitting and waistless, most of the line didn't need corsetry or padding. These garments were supposed to be more relaxed, which meant that the wearer was ready for anything.

This black faille cocktail dress is from the Spindle line and was one of the last dresses that Dior created.

CHRISTIAN
DIOR

04
LEGACY

"THE MAGIC NAME OF DIOR STANDS FOR FASHION TO THE MASSES. IT IS PART OF THE TAXI DRIVER'S VOCABULARY ...

"... AND IT IS OFTEN THE ONLY NAME THAT RINGS A FASHION BELL IN THE MIND OF THE AVERAGE MAN."

—Bettina Ballard, editor of *American Vogue*, from *Vogue on Dior*, 2012

or

THE SHOW MUST GO ON

Waiting in the wings at the House of Dior was the talented young fashion designer Yves Saint Laurent ...

CV

NAME: YVES HENRI DONAT MATHIEU-SAINT-LAURENT
BORN: ORAN, FRENCH ALGERIA
D.O.B: 1 AUGUST 1936

PERSONAL PROFILE:

An outcast who was bullied at school, Yves found solace in drawing and sketching. Obsessed with fashion, he made dresses for his sisters, and was fixated on becoming famous.

SKILLS:

- Forward thinking
- Creative
- Determined

EDUCATION & EMPLOYMENT

1952 As a teenager, Yves arrives in Paris and enrols at the Chambre Syndicale de la Haute Couture.

1953 Yves submits three sketches for a competition organized by the International Wool Secretariat and wins first place. The following year, Michel de Brunhoff, editor of *Vogue*, is impressed with his sketches and suggests he becomes a fashion designer.

1955 Yves is nearly 20 when he starts working for Christian Dior as a designer. By nature, he is reserved and it takes a while for his boss to notice his genius. Yves later said of Dior:

"HE TAUGHT ME THE BASIS OF MY ART ... I NEVER FORGOT THE YEARS I SPENT AT HIS SIDE."

1958–60

Yves creates six Dior collections but he is considered too daring for the traditional company.

1958 AUTUMN

Success is short and sweet: Yves' second collection is badly received. People begin to ask if haute couture has had its day.

1960

Yves is called up to the Algerian army to fight for independence. In his absence, the House of Dior terminates his contract.

1957 AUGUST

Christian Dior tells Yves' mother that he has chosen her son to be his successor.

....

Christian Dior tells his partner Jacques Rouet to groom Yves as his successor:

"ALL 40 OF HIS DESIGNS IN THE LAST COLLECTION WERE A HIT AND I WANT THE PAPERS TO KNOW ABOUT HIM."

....

24 OCTOBER

Christian Dior dies suddenly and Yves is appointed head designer at the House of Dior.

HE IS JUST 21 YEARS OLD!

1962 JANUARY

After a period of ill health, Yves bounces back with his own label and his first fashion show.

Yves becomes one of the leading lights of the fashion world. He keeps French style on the map in the decade when youth fashion explodes.

High points include the Mondrian dress and the Rive Gauche label with its catalogue of chic ready-to-wear costumes.

ON THE RED CARPET

1940s
MARLENE DIETRICH
The sultry starlet once said, "No Dior, no Dietrich" when discussing wardrobe for her films. She attended Dior's first show in 1947 and immediately ordered 10 dresses.

1950s
PRINCESS MARGARET
King George VI forbade his daughters from wearing the New Look. However, the young princess wore Dior's white dress to her 21st birthday in 1951 and proclaimed it, "My favourite dress of all."

1960s
MARILYN MONROE
Dior designed dresses that gloried in women's curves. Marilyn had enough front to wear an audacious backless dress specially designed for her by Dior.

1970s
GRACE KELLY
In her Hollywood heyday in the '50s, Grace Kelly had championed the New Look. By the '70s, the synced waist had been swapped for floaty, floor-length Dior creations, befitting her status as Princess Grace of Monaco.

1980s
ISABELLE ADJANI

The French film star became an ambassador for Dior in the 1980s. Colours were crazier, and Adjani wore an exotic number to attend the launch of the fragrance Poison in 1985.

1990s
LADY DIANA

Separated from Prince Charles and the strictures of the Royal Family, Princess Diana was freer in her wardrobe. She wore a Dior evening dress to attend Dior's 50th Anniversary in New York.

2000s
KATE MOSS

Supermodel Kate Moss chose Dior for the CFDA Awards in New York in 2005. The knee-length, corset-style cocktail dress was a modern twist on classic Dior. Moss went on to become the new face of its beauty range, Dior Addict.

2010s
RIHANNA

The pop princess has represented Dior on the red carpet. In 2016, Rihanna collaborated with Dior on its sunglasses collection.

LEGACY

HOUSE OF DIOR

The House of Dior has continued to create iconic looks and must-have accessories, many of which are endorsed and worn by the rich and famous ...

The Lady Dior features bejewelled D. I. O. R letters swinging from the top handle.

BAGS OF STYLE

The Lady Dior is a classic handbag, created by Dior in 1994. The following year, France's first lady, Bernadette Chirac, gave the bag – which was originally called Chouchou (French for favourite) – as a gift to Princess Diana. The princess was delighted and ordered it in every colour, and proceeded to be photographed everywhere she went with her favourite bag. Dior named the bag the Lady Dior in her honour.

EACH BAG TAKES **8** HOURS TO MAKE

PRICE: £3,100

APHRODISIAC AFTERSHAVE

The aftershave Eau Sauvage was launched by Dior in 1966 and smelt so divine that women started wearing it, too. The actor Steve McQueen was a huge fan and Johnny Depp has starred in the advertising campaign.

Part of its appeal is down to the addition of a chemical called Hedione (taken from the Greek word for fun, 'hedone') which has a jasmine-magnolia scent. Recently, scientists have discovered that Hedione activates parts of the brain associated with sexual attraction. In other words, Eau Sauvage really does have the power to turn women on!

THE EYES HAVE 'IT'

Dior has always been a label of choice for an 'It' girl. 21st-century It girl and singer Rihanna is not only a style ambassador for Dior but, in 2016, launched her own collection of eyewear in collaboration with the label. The range is called 'Rihanna' and it has a funky, ultra-modern edge which looks to the future and not the past.

Rihanna was involved in the creative process from start to finish; after looking through Dior's archives of eyewear, she got sketching before selecting the colours and materials for production. Rock-star looks don't come cheap:

EXCLUSIVE RIHANNA SUNGLASSES COST AROUND
£540

ET POUR HOMME?

Christian Dior menswear was opened in 1970 and by 1989 it accounted for 40 per cent of the House of Dior's business. Menswear boomed again when the label relaunched Dior Homme in 2000. That year, Brad Pitt wore one of the signature slim suits for his wedding to Jennifer Aniston. Stars like Mick Jagger and Kanye West have strutted their stuff in Dior Homme, too.

Slender suits still abound but designs are still experimental. In 2016, creative director Kris Van Assche looked to skate culture for ideas and English actor Robert Pattinson became the House's muse and model. In 2017, 60 years after the passing of Christian Dior, the 1980s club kid look was his inspiration.

MULTI-MEDIOR!

Flowers for Mrs Harris
By Paul Gallico
(Penguin, 1958)

Mrs Harris is a cleaner who lives in London. One day she falls in love with one of her rich client's Dior dress. When she wins £100 on the football pools Mrs Harris sets off for Paris in search of her own Dior outfit ...

Jeune Fille en Dior
(Young Girl in Dior)
Illustrated by Annie Goetzinger
(NBM Publishing, 2015)

Go behind the scenes and see what happened at the House of Dior in the days leading up to and beyond that fateful fashion show in February 1947, when Christian Dior introduced the New Look.

Mrs 'arris Goes to Paris (1992)

Angela Lansbury, Omar Sharif and Diana Rigg make the movie of the book *Flowers for Mrs Harris*.

Christian Dior: The Man Behind the Myth (2005)

A documentary about the young Christian Dior, directed by Philippe Lanfranchi.

Dior and I (2014)

A documentary, directed by Frédéric Tcheng, about creative director Raf Simons' first couture collection.

Christian Dior's legacy goes beyond just fashion. Here are some examples of where Christian has been immortalized in book, song and film.

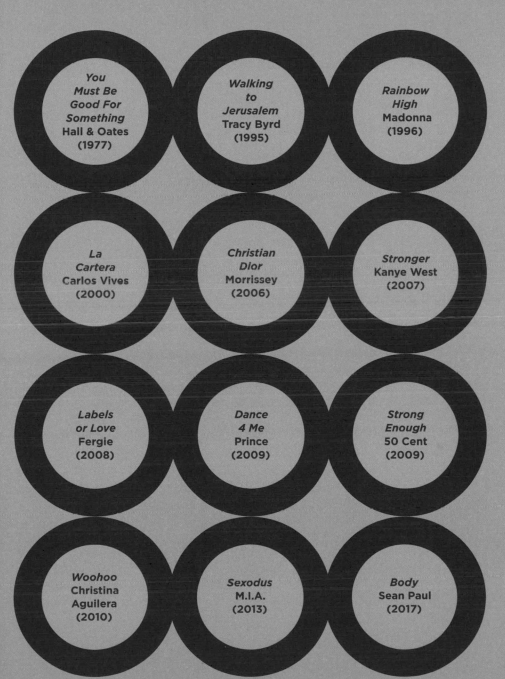

You Must Be Good For Something **Hall & Oates (1977)**

Walking to Jerusalem **Tracy Byrd (1995)**

Rainbow High **Madonna (1996)**

La Cartera **Carlos Vives (2000)**

Christian Dior **Morrissey (2006)**

Stronger **Kanye West (2007)**

Labels or Love **Fergie (2008)**

Dance 4 Me **Prince (2009)**

Strong Enough **50 Cent (2009)**

Woohoo **Christina Aguilera (2010)**

Sexodus **M.I.A. (2013)**

Body **Sean Paul (2017)**

A MEASURE OF TIME

1960
Marc Bohan is appointed creative director.

1980
The men's fragrance Jules is released.

1979
Dioressence perfume is launched.

1975
The Black Moon, the first Dior watch, is released.

1973
Christian Dior Ready-to-Wear Fur collection is started.

1984
Bernard Arnault buys the Willot Group, the owners of Dior.

1985
Poison perfume is first unleashed.

1989
Gianfranco Ferré becomes the first non-French head designer at the House of Dior.

2007
Kris Van Assche becomes artistic director for Dior Homme.

2005
Dior celebrates the 100th birthday of Christian Dior. At the Dior Museum, the exhibition 'Christian Dior: Man of the Century' is opened.

2002
Slimane is awarded 'International Designer of the Year'.

2007
The House of Dior celebrates its 60th Anniversary.

2011
John Galliano is fired for making anti-Semitic comments. Bill Gaytten succeeds him as artistic director.

2012
Fashion designer Raf Simons is appointed artistic director.

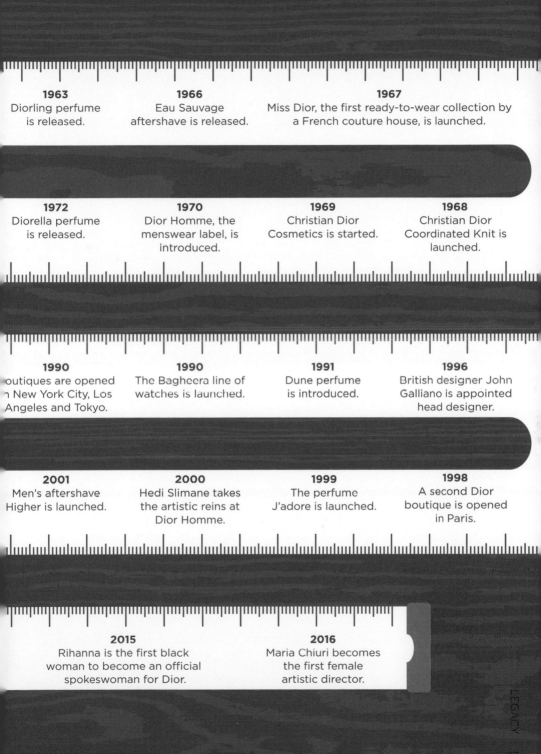

1963
Diorling perfume
is released.

1966
Eau Sauvage
aftershave is released.

1967
Miss Dior, the first ready-to-wear collection by
a French couture house, is launched.

1972
Diorella perfume
is released.

1970
Dior Homme, the
menswear label, is
introduced.

1969
Christian Dior
Cosmetics is started.

1968
Christian Dior
Coordinated Knit is
launched.

1990
outiques are opened
n New York City, Los
Angeles and Tokyo.

1990
The Bagheera line of
watches is launched.

1991
Dune perfume
is introduced.

1996
British designer John
Galliano is appointed
head designer.

2001
Men's aftershave
Higher is launched.

2000
Hedi Slimane takes
the artistic reins at
Dior Homme.

1999
The perfume
J'adore is launched.

1998
A second Dior
boutique is opened
in Paris.

2015
Rihanna is the first black
woman to become an official
spokeswoman for Dior.

2016
Maria Chiuri becomes
the first female
artistic director.

STAIRWAY TO SEVEN

Meet the seven creative directors who have left their mark on the hallowed stairway of the House of Dior at 30 avenue Montaigne ...

YVES SAINT LAURENT
1957–60

MARC BOHAN
1960–89

GIANFRANCO FERRÉ
1989–96

JOHN GALLIANO
1996–2011

BILL GAYTTEN
2011–2012

RAF SIMONS
2012–16

MARIA GRAZIA CHIURI
2016–PRESENT

Often referred to the as the last of the great French couturiers, Yves took over after Christian Dior's premature death. His first lines, which included triangular 'trapeze' dresses, were a hit but his beatnik-inspired 1960 collection, with its leather skirts and rollneck sweaters, signalled the end for him.

Marc arrived at Dior just as the Swinging Sixties began. His first collection was inspired by 1920s flappers, which appealed to the Dior customers. Even when fashion became more youth-orientated, Marc sided with tradition and elegance.

The Italian designer was a controversial choice to replace Bohan. With a background in architecture, his looks tended towards the geometric – which was sometimes at odds with traditional Dior. He believed his clothes were for a woman "who looked at tradition but was making her own choice."

The son of a plumber who halled from London was another surprising choice for the French couture house. However, he'd scooped British Designer of the Year on four occasions and his sense of drama and love of vintage style brought panache back to Dior.

British-born designer Bill Gaytten was unprepared for the role when he was appointed temporary head designer following Galliano's shock dismissal. After a rocky start, he soon settled into a more tailored and traditional look that was more wearable than some of Galliano's outlandish creations.

The son of a soldier and a cleaner, the Belgian designer was constantly compared to the great Christian Dior. Impeccable tailored suits and feminine flower dresses were back. Bringing in Rihanna and Jennifer Lawrence as style ambassadors was a touch of genius.

Dior's first female artistic director united girl power with the Dior dynasties in her vibrant and flirty collections: "We have to understand that it is possible to use the past in a modern way for modern women." In homage to Christian Dior, her first collection featured ball gowns embroidered with tarot card motifs.

TYPOGRAPHIC DIOR

Design Parfum

Toiles Christian Vogue Trapeze

Ava Gardner

Bar suit Les Rhumbs Flight

Maison Christian Dior

Princess Margaret Couture

Eau Sauvage Dieu et or Miss Dior Marlene Dietrich

Corolle
Dioressence
Fashion
Coco
Flatline
Diorama
30 avenue Montaigne
Couturier
Corsets
Dior
Lady Dior
Tarot
Organdie
Tulip
Eight
Cupola
New Look
Granville
God and gold
Lily of the Valley

BIOGRAPHIES

Ginette 'Catherine' Dior (1917–2008)

The youngest of the Dior children, Catherine was always Christian's favourite. During the Second World War, Catherine joined the Resistance and was awarded the Croix de Guerre medal for her service. Christian named the Miss Dior perfume after her.

Yves Saint Laurent (1936–2008)

An outcast who found solace in drawing, Yves was appointed head designer at the House of Dior at the age of 21. After the termination of his contract with Dior, he formed his own label in 1961 and became a leading light in the world of fashion.

Robert Piguet (1898–1953)

A swiss couturier who was famous for having trained Christian Dior, Hubert de Givenchy and Pierre Balmain, among others. Piguet opened the Piguet fashion house in Paris, which ran from 1933 until 1951, and hired Dior as an assistant in 1937.

Henri Sauguet (1901–89)

A French composer who became friends with Dior, bonding over their mutual love of music. With Pierre Gavotte and Jean Ozenne, they formed a group dubbed "Le Club" and frequented Parisian bars. Dior and Sauguet remained lifelong friends.

Raymonde Zehnacker (unknown)

Once characterized as "my second self," by Christian Dior, Madame Zehnacker was the directrice of the Dior design studio. Her role, in truth, expanded far beyond her title and Raymonde successfully ensured that the House of Dior was run to order.

Jacques Benita (unknown)

A singer from Algeria, Benita was the final lover of Christian Dior. The two met in 1956 and, despite being 30 years his senior, Christian began a close relationship with Benita until Diors' sudden death in 1957.

Jean Ozenne (1898–1969)
The cousin of Christian Bérard, Ozenne was a french fashion designer, illustrator and later an actor. Dior, while searching for work in Paris, lived with Ozenne who took note of his artistic talent and introduced him to the fashion world.

Mitzah Bricard (unknown)
Christian's great muse was also his chief stylist and advisor. Mitzah had a penchant for leopard print and statement jewellery. She rarely surfaced before 2 pm and when she did, she always wore a turban and a leopard print scarf around her wrist.

Jean Cocteau (1889–1963)
The French artist and writer, major figure of the early 20th-century avant garde. He was friends with Dior and they shared drinks in the cafés of Paris. Dior was inspired by the surrealist writer and paid homage to him, naming a white organdie dress after Cocteau.

Marie Madeleine Juliette Martin (1879–1931)
Christian's mother was born in Angers and moved to Granville to marry Maurice Dior. Christian inherited Marie's passion for fashion (on occasion, she designed her own dresses) and love of flowers. Inspirational yet formidable.

Christian Bérard (1902–1949)
More commonly known as Bébé, Bérard was a French artist, fashion illustrator and designer. After working for the Ballets Russes and as co-founder of the Ballets des Champs-Elysées, he illustrated for Chanel, Schiaparelli and Jean Patou.

Marcel Boussac (1889–1980)
A French entrepreneur who made his money in the textile industry, Boussac financed the House of Dior in 1946. The Boussac group was declared bankrupt in 1978 and the House of Dior was bought by the Willot Group.

● family
● friend
● colleague
● companion

INDEX

DIOR BY NUMBERS

8 LUCKY NUMBER

Christian gave one of his debut lines the name '8' because the tiny waist, the enhanced hips and the bigger bust looked a little like the figure eight.

The House of Dior was founded in the 8th arrondissement of Paris, in an eight-storey building with eight workshops, on 8 October 1946.

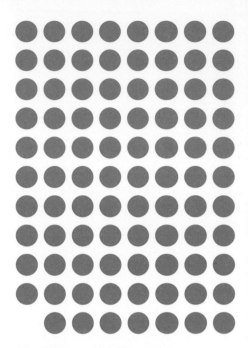

12 DRESSES

Movie stars adored gowns by Monsieur Dior. In 1956, Christian designed a dozen dresses for the actress Ava Gardner for her film *The Little Hut*.

87 COUNTRIES

By 1957, Christian Dior had conquered the world, with licenses issued to places as far flung as Australia, USA, Cuba and Britain.

100,000 CREATIONS

By 1956, the 10th anniversary of the House of Dior, the company had created thousands of garments and was turning over $20 million a year.